D0497814

This book is dedicated to
Chelsea Petrova-Dachshund.
A very small dog with
a very big heart.

THIS BOOK
BELONGS TO

MASON
& RYE

from Grammie

"Finse Explores Russia"

The right of Karine Hagen to be identified as the author
and Suzy-Jane Tanner to be identified as the illustrator
of this work has been asserted by them in accordance
with the Copyright Designs and Patents Act 1988.

Text copyright © Karine Hagen 2014
Illustrations copyright © Suzy-Jane Tanner 2014

First published by Viking Cruises
83 Wimbledon Park Side, London, SW19 5LP

ISBN 978-1-909968-03-5

www.finse.me

Reproduction, printing and binding by Colophon Digital Projects Ltd,
Brentford, TW8 8LB, United Kingdom

FINSE
EXPLORES RUSSIA

Karine Hagen
Suzy-Jane Tanner

FINLAND

Lake Lado

St Petersburg

ESTONIA

LATVIA

FINSE
EXPLORES
RUSSIA

Kizhi Island

N

Lake Onega

Volga-Baltic Waterway

RUSSIA

Uglich

Volga River

Yaroslavl

Volga River

Moscow Canal

Moscow

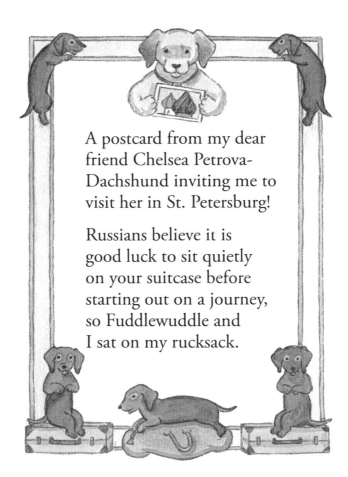

A postcard from my dear
friend Chelsea Petrova-
Dachshund inviting me to
visit her in St. Petersburg!

Russians believe it is
good luck to sit quietly
on your suitcase before
starting out on a journey,
so Fuddlewuddle and
I sat on my rucksack.

Russia is a huge country, so I decided to explore some of it.

I arrived in Moscow, the capital city.

I don't think the guard dogs at the Kremlin are allowed to smile at all!

When Russia was part of the Soviet Union, famous Moscow dogmanauts Belka and Strelka took part in the space programme.

In many metro stations there are beautiful statues. I rubbed the guard dog statue's nose for luck.

Russians love music.

The balalaika is an instrument made in many different sizes.

I watched a performance of Tchaikovsky's Swan Lake by the talented and elegant dancers of the Borzoi ballet.

11

There were lots of
travellers from all
over the world in
Red Square.

Fuddlewuddle and I
visited the magnificent
St. Basil's Cathedral.

Then it was time
to set out down
the Volga River.

Russia is so far north that during the summer, the sun barely sets.

I visited a typical dacha, a summerhouse on the banks of the Volga River.

Everyone grows fruit and vegetables to make jams and pickles for the winter months.

But in the Russian winter, the sun barely rises.

It is time to stay snug indoors. Sometimes we play chess.

The river freezes so everyone wraps up warmly when they do go out to play.

Uglich is one of the prettiest towns in Russia.

I bought flowers from babushka Nadya.

Then I had tea made on a traditional samovar, with a local family.
I tasted the delicious pickles they had made.

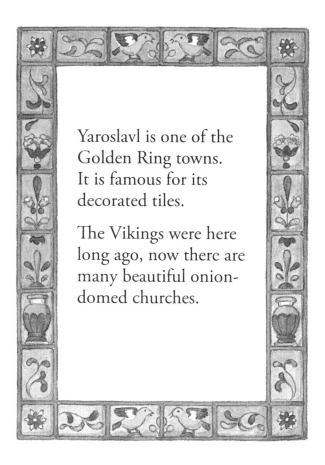

Yaroslavl is one of the
Golden Ring towns.
It is famous for its
decorated tiles.

The Vikings were here
long ago, now there are
many beautiful onion-
domed churches.

On Kizhi Island I took a walking tour through the Open Air Museum.

I saw an old windmill but, best of all, I liked the fairytale wooden church. It was built in 1714 without a single nail, and has 22 domes!

When I reached
St. Petersburg, it was lovely
to see my friend Chelsea.

The city is famous for its
many canals and bridges.

We sailed down the Moika
Canal to see the Church
of Our Saviour on the
Spilled Blood.

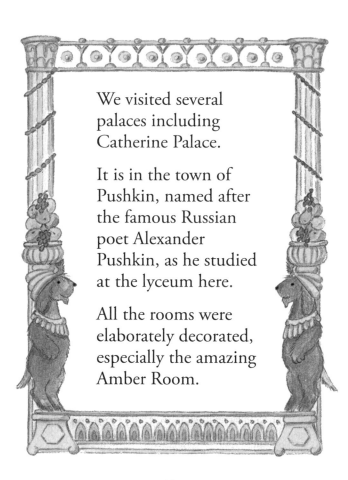

We visited several palaces including Catherine Palace.

It is in the town of Pushkin, named after the famous Russian poet Alexander Pushkin, as he studied at the lyceum here.

All the rooms were elaborately decorated, especially the amazing Amber Room.

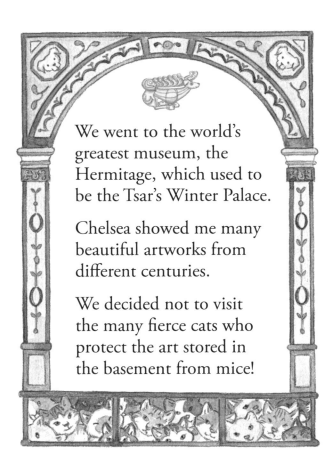

We went to the world's greatest museum, the Hermitage, which used to be the Tsar's Winter Palace.

Chelsea showed me many beautiful artworks from different centuries.

We decided not to visit the many fierce cats who protect the art stored in the basement from mice!

Chelsea gave me a set of matryoshka dogs to remember my trip.

I was sad to say goodbye and leave Russia.

But I was looking forward to my next adventure!

DOGOLOGY

As well as her dear friend Chelsea, Finse met many new canine friends in Russia. Here are some of them: